Copyright © 2020 by

Unique Designs Print

...ghts reserved. No part of this publication may be ...oduced, distributed, or transmitted in any form or ...any means, without the permission of the publisher.

Are you enjoying
this awesome book?

if so, please leave us a review. We are very
interested in your feedback to create even
better products for you to enjoy in
the near future.

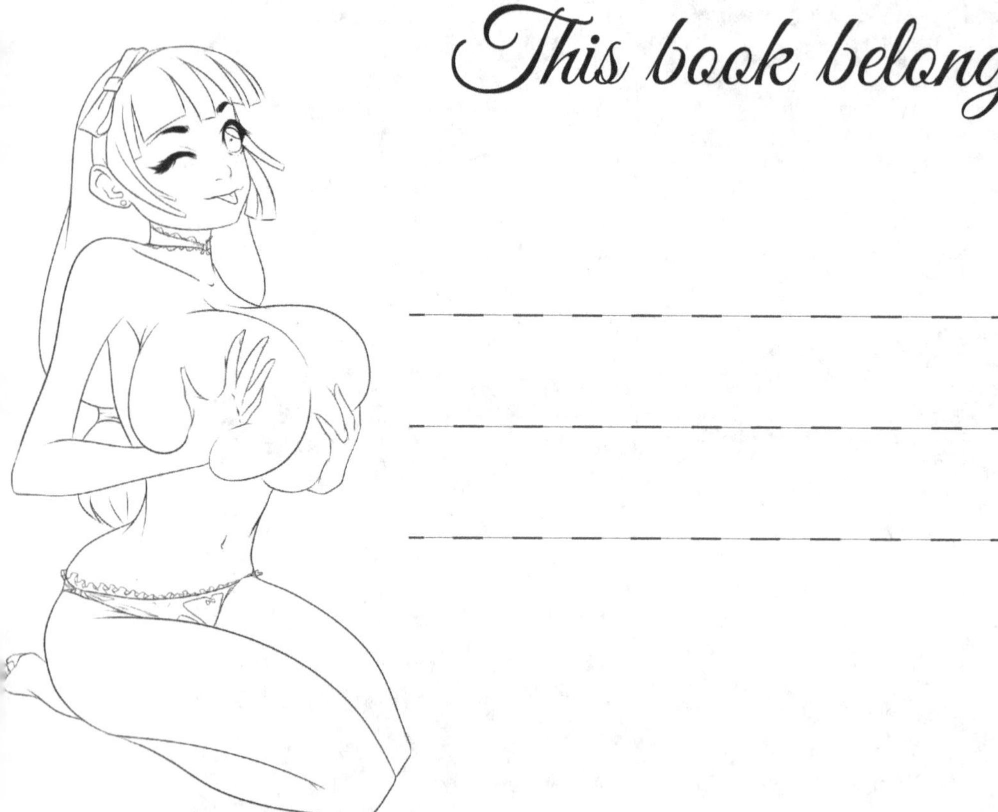

This book belongs to:

____

____

____

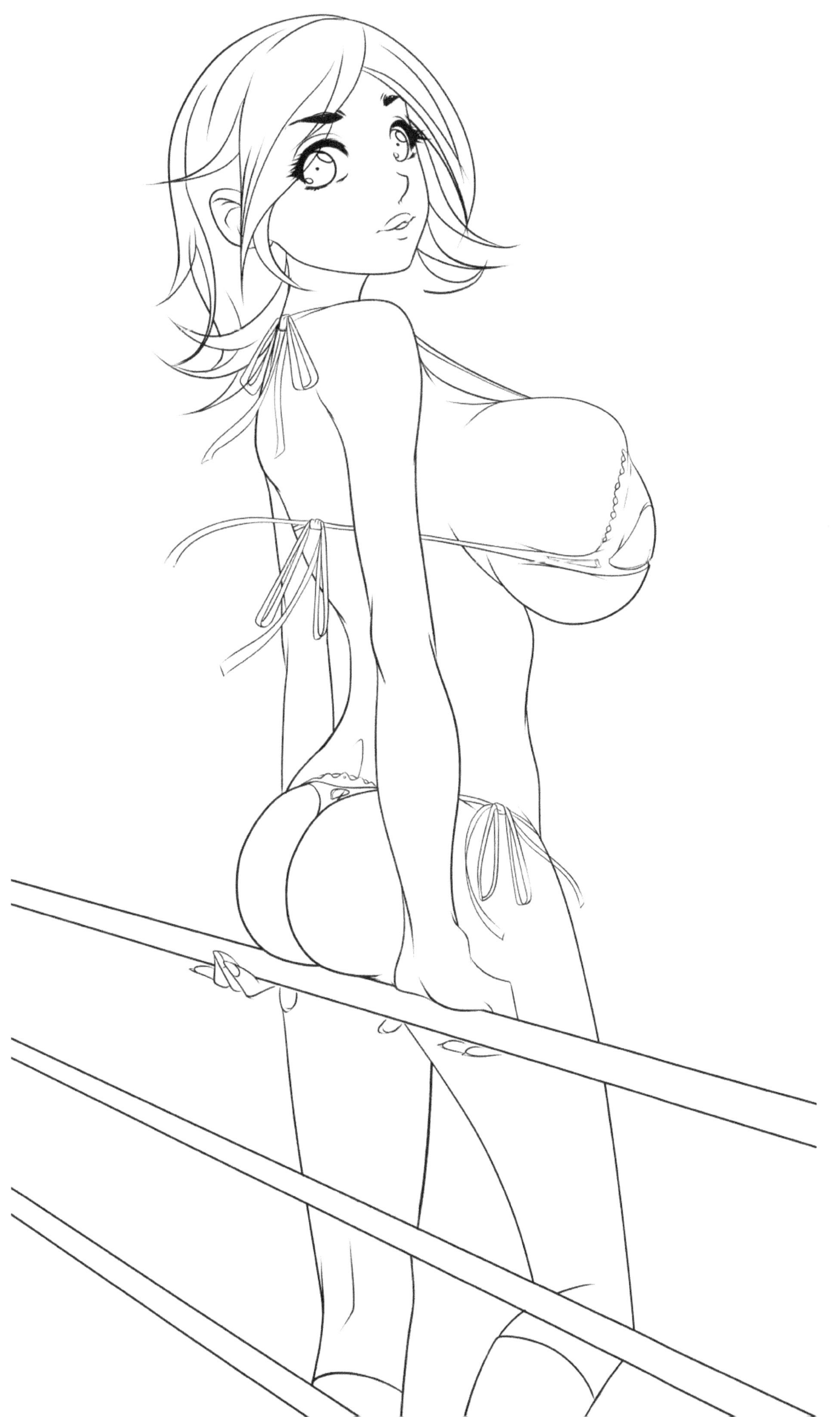

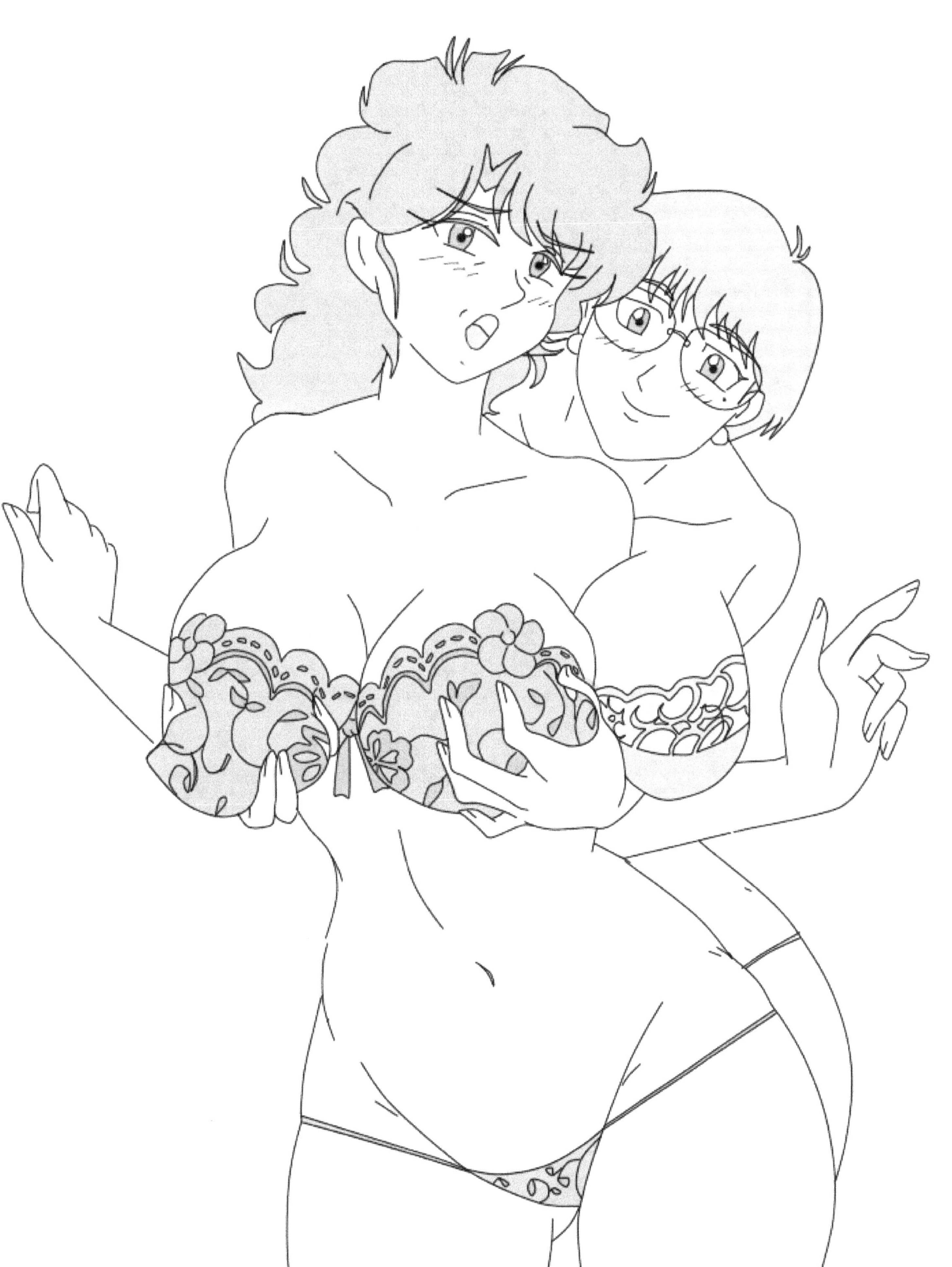

サアラ

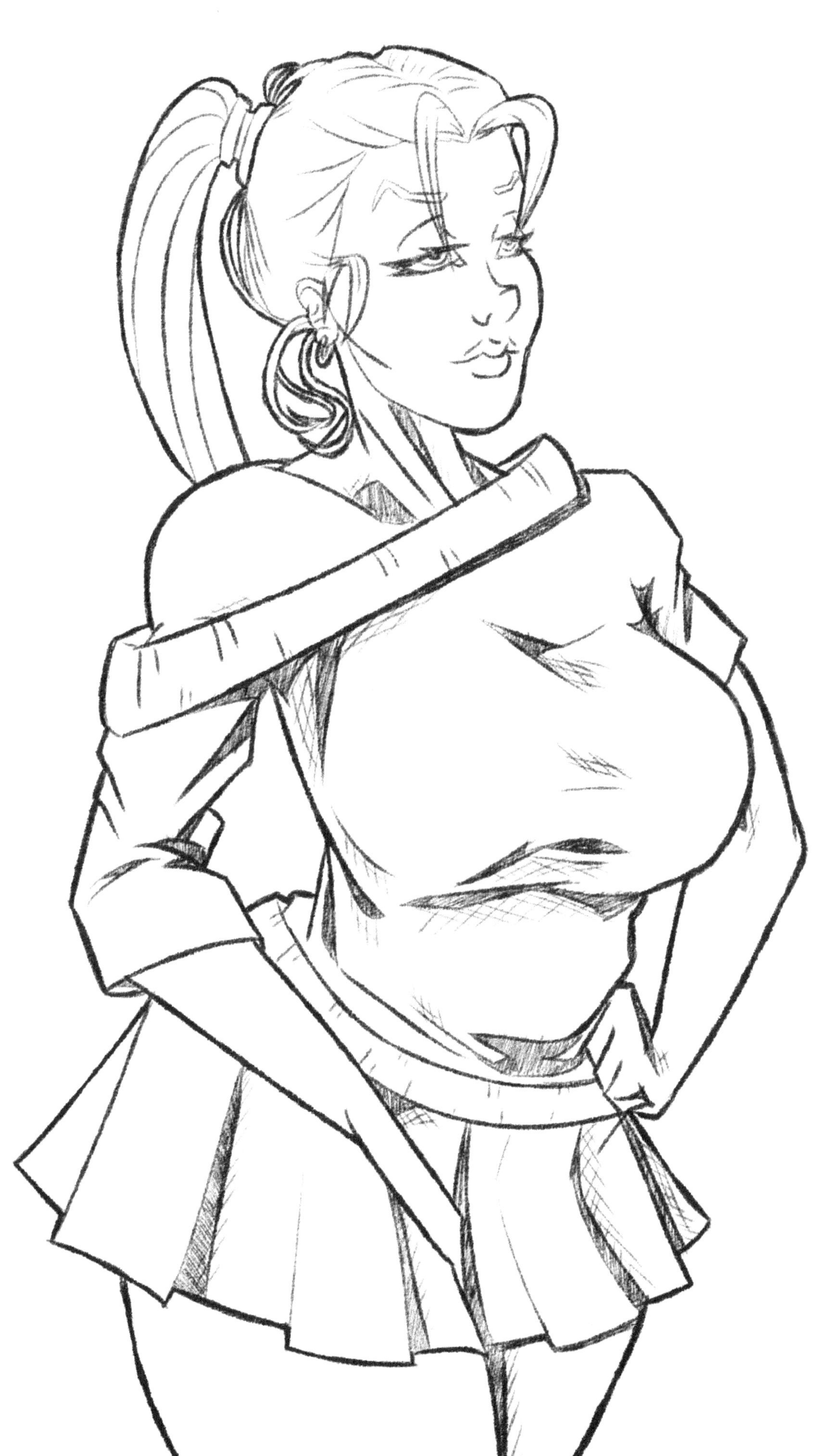

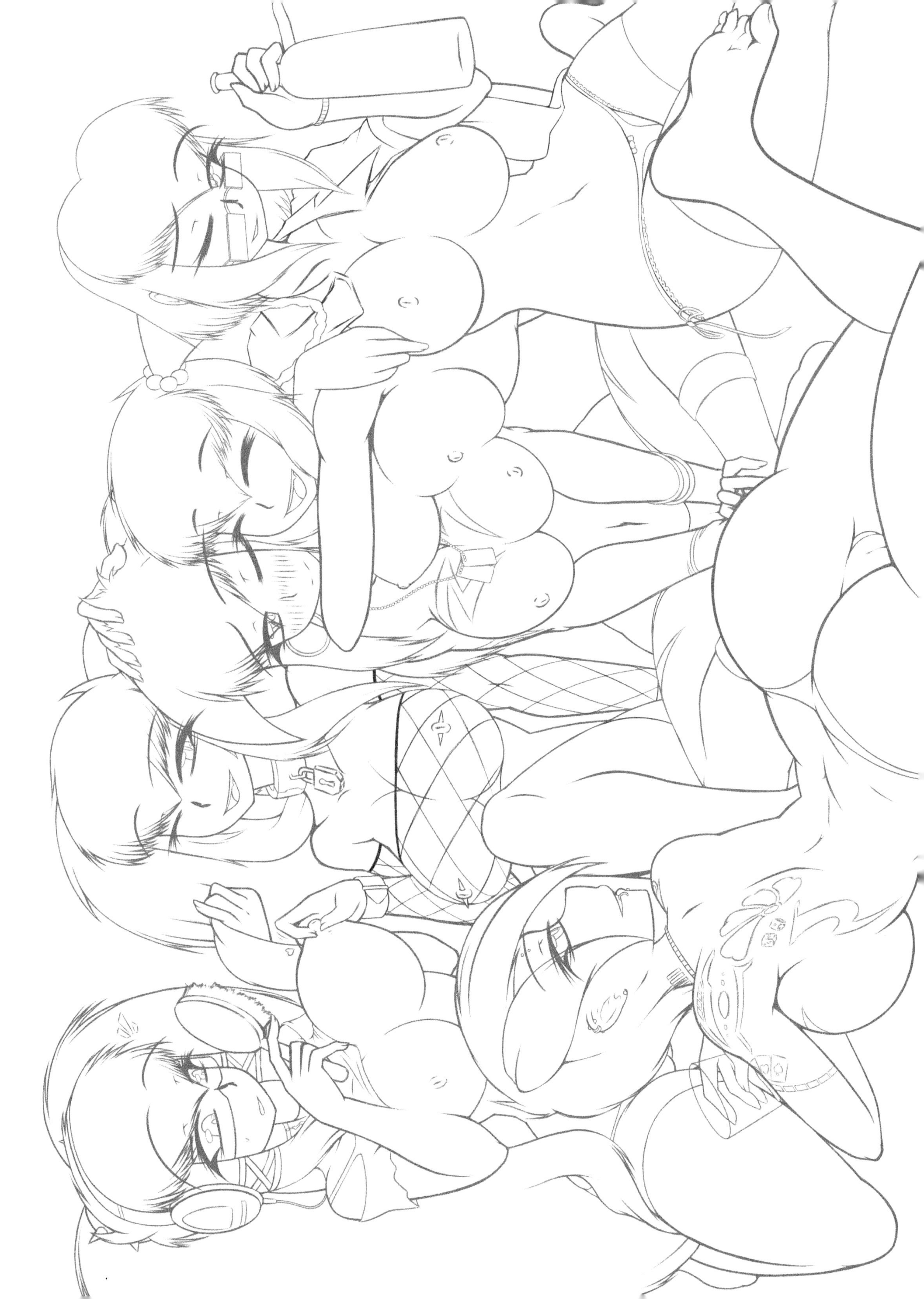

www.ingramcontent.com/pod-product-compliance
Lightning Source LLC
Chambersburg PA
CBHW081444250726
48662CB00009B/2942

9 798648 324602